IRON WILL

SURVIVING THE STORM

Kristin J. Russo

Surviving the Storm
Iron Will

Copyright © 2020
Published by Full Tilt Press
Written by Kristin J. Russo
All rights reserved.

Printed in the United States of America.
No part of this book may be reproduced in any manner whatsoever without written permission, except in the case of brief quotations embodied in critical articles and reviews.

Full Tilt Press
42982 Osgood Road
Fremont, CA 94539
readfulltilt.com

Full Tilt Press publications may be purchased for educational, business, or sales promotional use.

Editorial Credits
Design and layout by Sara Radka
Edited by Lauren Dupuis-Perez
Copyedited by Renae Gilles

Image Credits
FEMA: Jocelyn Augustino, 9, 44 (top); Getty Images: Colin Anderson Productions pty ltd, cover, doram, 36 (canned food), Mario Tama, 11, TEK IMAGE, 36 (first aid kit), Xuanyu Han, background; NASA: Jeff Schmaltz, 22; Newscom: KRT, 31, 35, Polaris/Michael Stravato, 17, UPI/Air National Guard/Staff Sgt. Daniel J. Martinez, 15, UPI/Jerome Hicks, 16; Pixabay: 12019, 1, 470906, 37 (axe), Comfreak, 4, denvit, 36 (water), Free-Photos, 2 (top), JosepMonter, 37 (radio), TheDigitalArtist, 2 (bottom), Vasil360, 38, 39, WikimediaImages, 36 (can opener), 37 (flashlight); U.S. Air Force: Staff Sgt. Kelly Goonan, 43; U.S. Coast Guard: Lt.j.g Earl Lingerfelt, 33; U.S. Navy: Mass Communication Specialist 1st Class Peter D. Blair, 23; Wikimedia: ABI image captured by NOAA's GOES-16 satellite, 13, Infrogmation, 34, Library of Congress/Griffith & Griffith, 3 (bottom), 27, 44 (bottom), M.H. Zahner, 28, NASA image courtesy Jeff Schmaltz, MODIS Land Rapid Response Team at NASA GSFC, 3 (top), 7, NOAA, 10, 25, 29, Trócaire/Caritas/Eoghan Rice, 3 (middle), 19, 21

ISBN: 978-1-62920-805-3 (library binding)
ISBN: 978-1-62920-821-3 (eBook)

CONTENTS

Surviving the Storm 4
Brave Escape 6
Baby on Board 12
Nightmare Storm 18
A Storm's Witness 24
The Prepared 30
The Stuff of Survival 36
Iron Will Stats 38
Map: Deadly Storms 40
Iron Will 42
      Quiz 44
      Activity 45
      Glossary 46
      Read More 47
      Internet Sites 47
      Index 48

SURVIVING THE STORM

Years ago, a hurricane could strike without warning. A monster storm would form at sea. It would crash into land. Floods and brutal winds destroyed entire communities. There was little time for people to prepare for such a disaster. Since then, there have been advances in **technology**. **Meteorologists** can warn people when a dangerous storm is headed their way. But this doesn't always help. Some people can't—or won't—**evacuate**. Climate change continues to produce more frequent and stronger hurricanes and typhoons. It is important for people to have the knowledge—and **iron will**— to survive a monster storm.

technology: tools and knowledge used to meet a need or solve a problem

meteorologist: a scientist who studies weather and weather patterns

evacuate: to leave a dangerous place

iron will: having a strong feeling that you are going to do something and that you will not allow anything to stop you

SURVIVING THE STORM

BRAVE ESCAPE

Jaimie Cummings
Hurricane Katrina
New Orleans, Louisiana
2005

Tropical Storm Katrina was set to dump a lot of rain and wind on the Bahamas on August 24, 2005. It was not yet a deadly hurricane.

"Dead bodies from the cemetery were floating in the water, along with other people who had just drowned."

JAIMIE CUMMINGS

It was August 23, 2005. Meteorologists saw a storm forming in the Atlantic Ocean. Five days later, it had doubled in size. It was called Katrina, and it was a Category 5 hurricane. This is the strongest and fiercest type of hurricane. Katrina reached wind speeds of 172 miles (278 kilometers) per hour. But Katrina's wind speeds weakened by the time it made landfall on August 29. Many thought this was good news. Then the **storm surge** arrived.

Katrina's storm surge was 27.8 feet (8.4 meters) high and 20 miles (32 km) wide. It was one of the most damaging storm surges to hit the US. When Katrina struck, Jaimie Cummings, 14, was visiting her mother. They were at Memorial Baptist Hospital in New Orleans, Louisiana. Jaimie and her mother ran to the hallway as brutal winds smashed the windows. They panicked as floodwaters rose at a deadly speed. They decided to leave the hospital.

storm surge: a rising of the sea as a result of atmospheric pressure changes and wind associated with a storm

SURVIVING THE STORM

WATER RESCUE

Outside the hospital, Jaimie saw something that gave her hope. Police officers were arriving at the hospital in boats. They were coming to save as many people as they could. Jaimie and her mother found seats on one of those police boats. They traveled through dangerous floodwaters to safety. "Dead bodies from the cemetery were floating in the water, along with other people who had just drowned," Jaimie said.

Jaimie and her mother were lucky to find a way out. About 1.2 million people were ordered to evacuate before the storm hit. But many stayed in New Orleans. Some had no **transportation**. Many others had nowhere to go. Thousands of people took shelter in the Superdome, an athletic stadium. Living conditions were harsh inside the shelter. The storm knocked out power and ripped off a roof panel. Three people died there.

transportation: a way to get from one place to another, usually in a vehicle of some sort

By September 3, 2005, FEMA volunteers had evacuated 25,000 people from affected areas. They saved about 11,500 lives.

SURVIVING THE STORM 9

SAFE IN TEXAS

Jaimie and her mother did not go to the Superdome. They made it out of the city by boat and out of the state by helicopter. They went to the Reese Center in Lubbock, Texas. Red Cross volunteers took care of them there.

Jaimie had no time to pack a suitcase before she and her mother fled. Volunteers at the Reese Center gave her clothing and personal items. These had been part of donations that had poured in from around the country. Before the terrible storm, Jaimie had lived with her mother and her aunt's family in the 17th Ward in New Orleans. After four days in Texas, she learned that their neighborhood had been destroyed. She could not go home.

Jaimie and her family survived a storm that killed 1,833 people. Jaimie ultimately settled in a town called Ruston, Louisiana, and never again lived in her old neighborhood in the 17th Ward.

RECORD STORM SURGE

Hurricane Katrina was shaped like a lopsided doughnut. It suctioned water from the ocean on its dense right side. This water fell as rain once the storm made landfall. This created a storm surge four times as large as the previous record-holder, Hurricane Camille, which drenched Louisiana in 1969.

More than 20,000 stranded victims of Hurricane Katrina lived in the Superdome for days after the hurricane had passed.

THE UNITED STATES

KANSAS
MISSOURI
KENTUCKY
TENNESSEE
OKLAHOMA
ARKANSAS
MISSISSIPPI
ALABAMA
★ Lubbock
★ Ruston
TEXAS
LOUISIANA
★ New Orleans

Area affected by Hurricane Katrina

SURVIVING THE STORM 11

BABY ON BOARD

The Smiths
Hurricane Harvey
Houston, Texas
2017

12 IRON WILL

On August 25, 2017, Hurricane Harvey was at its strongest. Satellite images show a clear spiral and central eye to the storm.

It was the summer of 2017. Annie and Greg Smith had just settled into their new home in Houston, Texas. The Smiths had moved from Virginia to Houston. Both Annie and Greg were training to be doctors at a Houston hospital. The couple had even more exciting plans—preparing for the birth of their first child.

Meanwhile, Hurricane Harvey began to take shape over the Atlantic Ocean. On August 25, the monster storm slammed into Texas. It reached wind speeds of 132 miles (212 km) per hour. Harvey dumped more than 4 feet (1.2 m) of rain on Houston. Floodwaters crept up to the Smith's front door. Then, Annie went into labor. Annie, Greg, and their soon-to-be-born baby would need an iron will to survive what came next.

"Around the time we saw the flooding on our street and parking lot, I went into active labor and started having frequent, painful contractions."

ANNIE SMITH

SURVIVING THE STORM 13

RECORD FLOODING

Hurricane Harvey brought more rain to Houston than the city normally receives in a year. The streets were **impassable** in the raging flood. The hospital was only 2 miles (3.2 km) away from the Smiths' home. But there was no way the couple could drive there.

"Around the time we saw the flooding on our street and parking lot, I went into active labor," Annie said. She "started having frequent, painful contractions." The couple called for help. But the city's 911 system was overwhelmed. Their calls were not answered. Annie and Greg were on their own.

They prepared to deliver their baby at home. They asked their new neighbors for help. Many people who lived in their apartment building worked as doctors and nurses. But there was no one there who specialized in delivering babies. Neighbors gathered surgical tools, **sterile** bandages, and other supplies that they thought the couple might need.

---

impassable: not able to be passed, traveled, or crossed

sterile: clean of bacteria

Harvey caused about $125 billion in damage. The flooding caused the most damage and the weight of the water temporarily sunk the city by 0.8 inches (2 centimeters).

SURVIVING THE STORM 15

COMMUNITY SUPPORT

Then, the Smiths had a stroke of luck. One of Annie's colleagues contacted a family member. They lived next door to a Houston fire station. Soon Greg saw a dump truck pull up in front of their home. Help had arrived!

Houston firefighters planned to drive Anna through the flooded streets to the hospital. An ambulance would float away in the floodwaters. But a heavy dump truck with large tires might just make it. The neighbors waded into the water. They formed a human chain. They joined arms and guided Anna and Greg toward the truck. They kept the couple from slipping away in the **torrent**.

"I was sitting on a fire hose with a shower curtain over my head to protect me from the rain, having powerful contractions every four minutes," Annie said. The couple made it to the hospital in time. A short while later, their daughter, Adrielle, was born. Both mother and baby were safe and healthy after the delivery.

ANSWERING THE CALL

First responders answered 10,000 calls for help during Hurricane Harvey. About 30,000 people fled the area before the hurricane hit. More than 80 people died due to high winds and flooding during the storm.

torrent: a strong, fast-moving stream of water; a flood

16 IRON WILL

Many of those helping to rescue trapped victims of Hurricane Harvey were neighbors and members of local fire and rescue organizations.

THE UNITED STATES

TENNESSEE
ARKANSAS
OKLAHOMA
NEW MEXICO
MISSISSIPPI
ALABAMA
TEXAS
LOUISIANA
★ Houston

Area affected by Hurricane Harvey

SURVIVING THE STORM 17

NIGHTMARE STORM

The Pasi Family
Super Typhoon Yolanda
Tacloban, Philippines
2013

Super Typhoon Yolanda completely destroyed many homes. Homes that had stood for a generation were no longer standing after the typhoon.

"If I allowed myself to be afraid, my son would die, my family would starve."

LANCE PASI

Tacloban is a city in the province of Leyte, Philippines. Katherine and Warren Pasi were residents there. They had to make a difficult decision. They decided that Katherine would move north to Manila to work in a call center. Warren would stay home with their four sons. Unfortunately, they had not predicted Super Typhoon Yolanda.

Yolanda hit the Philippines on November 8, 2013. It was one of strongest storms ever recorded on Earth. Wind gusts reached up to 235 miles (380 km) per hour. The storm knocked out power and all communication to Tacloban. The city was home to more than 200,000 people. Katherine saw on the news that her hometown was in trouble. High winds and floodwaters destroyed an evacuation center and killed hundreds of people inside. Katherine feared that her family had all died. Only an iron will could have saved them.

A FAMILY SEPARATED

Katherine raced to the airport. She wanted to fly to Leyte so she could find her family. No one would take her. It was too dangerous.

While Katherine was trying to reach her family, Warren and his sons struggled to survive. Warren gave his younger sons helmets to wear. He hoped this would protect them from falling debris. Hope turned into terror when the 20-foot (6-m) storm surge flooded their home. Eleven-year-old Karl, the youngest boy, couldn't swim. The floodwaters stopped rising just as they reached Karl's chin.

Katherine and Warren's adult son, Lance, stayed with his wife and baby in the two-story home of a relative. Punishing winds tore the house apart while they were inside. When the storm calmed, the home had only one room left—the one protecting his family and 11 more frightened people. "I told my wife we're done for. If this room gives, we all would have died," said Lance.

Katherine, alone in Manila, was losing hope. After three long days, she finally received a text. "Ma, we're all alive." It was from Lance. He had sent the message on a borrowed phone.

Super Typhoon Yolanda caused $2.2 billion in damage.

SURVIVING THE STORM 21

THE AFTERMATH

The streets of Tacloban were littered with debris and dead bodies. There was no food and no clean water to drink. "People were no longer normal. They would do anything just to eat. Even killing others. I also looted a grocery store. I got food, milk. If I allowed myself to be afraid, my son would die, my family would starve," said Warren.

Warren and his sons went to the airport. They hoped to find seats on one of the C-130 military planes that were flying survivors away from the city. There was no food or water at the overcrowded airport. After waiting in line for three days, the family gave up and left. Days later, they returned to the airport to try again. With help from a friend who was also a policeman, they found seats on a flight to Manila. Finally, Katherine, Warren, and their sons were together again. Super Typhoon Yolanda claimed 6,340 lives, but the Pasi family was safe.

HURRICANES, TYPHOONS, AND CYCLONES

Hurricanes and typhoons are the same type of storm. They are tropical cyclones. A tropical cyclone is an organized system of clouds and thunderstorms that rotates, or moves in a circle. The hole in the center of the circle is called the "eye" of the storm. A hurricane is a tropical cyclone that forms in the Atlantic Ocean, and a typhoon is a tropical cyclone that forms in the Pacific Ocean.

Huge cargo planes transported survivors from destroyed areas in the Philippines. The American military relief efforts became known as Operation Damayan.

THE PHILIPPINES

★ Tacloban, Leyte

Area affected by Super Typhoon Yolanda

SURVIVING THE STORM 23

A STORM'S WITNESS

Richard Spillane
Great Galveston Hurricane
Texas
1900

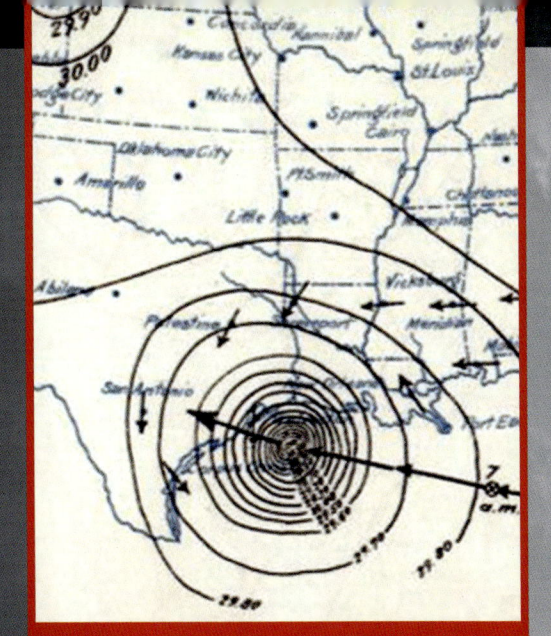

Before satellite imagery, newspapers relied on hand drawn weather maps from meteorologists.

"To leave a house was to drown."

RICHARD SPILLANE

The years leading up to 1900 were a time of wealth and prosperity for the people of Galveston, Texas. The town was home to about 38,000 people in September 1900. Galveston had the first telephone in the state. It was also the first town in Texas to have electricity installed. The Gulf of Mexico attracted many visitors. People in poor health would bathe in the warm water to feel better and get well. The port at Galveston was one of the richest in the country.

Then, on September 8, 1900, reports came in from nearby ships. A storm was coming. But people did not want to leave. Richard Spillane, editor of the *Galveston Tribune*, was among those who stayed. Only his iron will saved him. By nightfall on that terrible day, the city was completely underwater.

SURVIVING THE STORM   25

FEAR AND DEATH

The winds were terrible. They ripped apart buildings and knocked down telegraph poles. However, Spillane wrote that the storm surge was the most terrifying part. People tried to run to safety, but it did no good. "During all this time, the people of Galveston were like rats in traps," Spillane wrote. "The highest portion of the city was 4 to 5 feet [1.2 to 1.5 m] underwater." But in most cases, "the streets were submerged to a depth of 10 feet [3 m]."

Those who tried to flee had nowhere to go. "To leave a house was to drown," Spillane wrote. Galveston was a small island. It was only about 5 feet (1.5 m) above sea level. The storm surge carried tidal waves higher than 15 feet (4.5 m). People and animals tried to swim for their lives. Some survived on the top floors of buildings—but only as long as those buildings didn't collapse.

Galveston was never able to recover fully from the hurricane. It killed between 6,000 and 8,000 people. Not all of the homes and businesses were able to be rebuilt.

SURVIVING THE STORM

FINDING HELP

Spillane survived. He fled as soon as he could. City officials sent him to spread news of the devastation. They wanted him to ask for help. Spillane needed to send information about the disaster to the *New York Times*. He hoped news would spread quickly and much-needed help would soon arrive.

Spillane traveled by foot, boat, and train to Houston. It was about 45 miles (72 km) away. He sent his first telegraph to the *New York Times* on September 10. His story detailed the terrible tragedy. No building was left unharmed. Thousands of victims had been swept out to sea.

News of the terrible storm spread. The country was quick to act. Tents and food supplies were shipped to survivors. But some supplies didn't make it. One train carrying supplies had to turn back because the tracks to Galveston were "blocked by lumber, debris, pianos, trunks, and dead bodies." The city of Galveston was rebuilt on a much smaller scale. But the city never fully recovered.

DEADLIEST

The Great Galveston Hurricane took place before hurricanes and typhoons were given names. People who live in the region call it the Great Storm of 1900. With wind speeds of 145 miles (233 km) per hour, the storm was a Category 4 hurricane. Between 6,000 and 8,000 people were killed. About 10,000 were left homeless by the storm. It remains the deadliest hurricane in US history.

About 3,600 buildings were demolished by the storm.

THE UNITED STATES

- TENNESSEE
- OKLAHOMA
- ARKANSAS
- NEW MEXICO
- MISSISSIPPI
- ALABAMA
- TEXAS
- LOUISIANA
- ★ Galveston

Area affected by the Great Galveston Hurricane

SURVIVING THE STORM 29

A BIG MISTAKE

As Katrina bore down on Mississippi and Louisiana, Jackson started to regret her decision to stay in Gulfport. Watching the news, she learned that the eye of the storm was headed straight for them. "I said to everyone, 'I want you to forgive me now, because I think I made a mistake. I'm afraid we're all going to have to fight very hard not to die.'"

In the early hours of Monday morning, Jackson heard the first of the treacherous winds. She had been keeping a close eye on a large tree in her neighbor's yard. Before long, she heard a sickening crack. "Run!" she yelled. The group ran to a closet in the center of the house and made it to safety just before the tree crashed through the roof.

High winds caused the air pressure to build inside of the house. The walls began to heave. They raced to open the windows to release the pressure. No one was home to open the windows in the house next door. They saw it explode.

About 90 percent of the buildings along the Biloxi-Gulfport coastline were destroyed by the storm surge.

DESTRUCTION

When the sun came up, everyone in their group was still alive. But the surrounding neighborhood had been demolished. Downed power lines and debris covered the roads. Jackson tried to drive to her own house. But she had to walk the last 3 miles (5 km) because the roads were impassable. "When we turned toward my street, all I saw was a big lake where there once had been houses, trees, and roads," she said.

Jackson lost her home and all of her possessions except for a few items she found while digging in the mud. But she considered herself lucky. The storm killed an entire family who lived in her neighborhood. But she and her loved ones were safe.

EVACUATION PLANS

A hurricane warning means that hurricane conditions are expected. Meteorologists issue a warning when they believe that a storm with wind speeds higher than 74 miles (119 km) per hour will hit a certain area within 36 hours. People under a hurricane warning should find shelter in their homes or emergency centers, or evacuate as soon as possible if they can.

34 IRON WILL

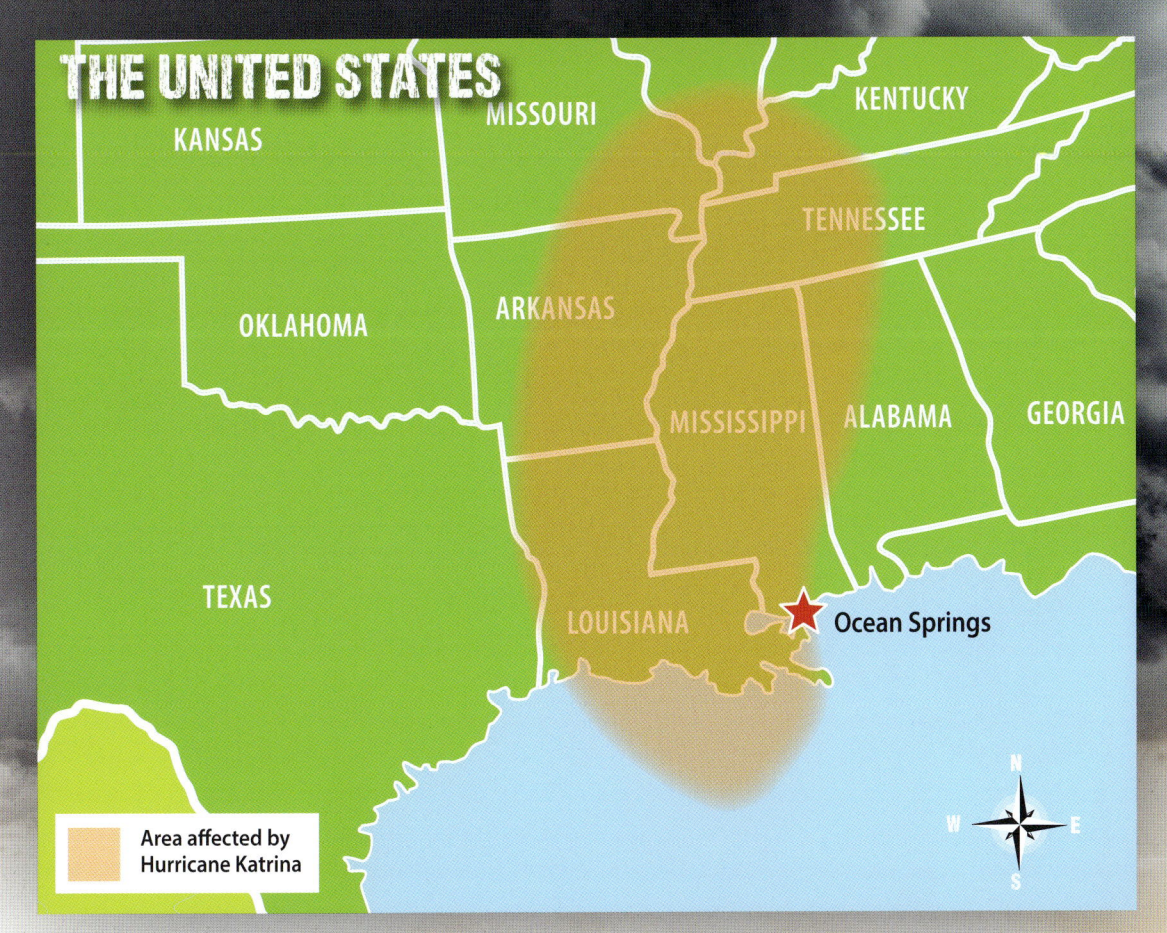

Hurricane Katrina's 28-foot storm surge also wiped out bridges and streets. Only the support beams were left of a bridge on US Highway 90.

THE UNITED STATES

KANSAS • MISSOURI • KENTUCKY • TENNESSEE • OKLAHOMA • ARKANSAS • MISSISSIPPI • ALABAMA • GEORGIA • TEXAS • LOUISIANA

★ Ocean Springs

Area affected by Hurricane Katrina

SURVIVING THE STORM 35

THE STUFF OF SURVIVAL

Surviving major storms is not easy. Even simple supplies can help people survive while they wait for rescue. These are some of the resources that can help save lives.

FIRST AID KIT
A first aid kit is a collection of supplies to help people who are sick or injured during an emergency. Most first aid kits hold bandages, sterile gauze, antibiotic ointment, and other medications or supplies that families might need.

BOTTLED WATER
Floodwaters can contaminate tap water. Electrical outages can knock out well pumps. Having bottled water on hand is important to keep hydrated and healthy.

CANNED FOOD AND A CAN OPENER
Canned food is safe to eat if the food in the refrigerator or pantry is damaged in the storm. A can opener is required if the cans do not have pull tabs.

FLASHLIGHT
Electrical outages knock out lights. When night falls, storm victims need flashlights with fresh batteries to see.

BATTERY-OPERATED RADIO
Strong winds can knock out electricity and Wi-Fi. A battery-operated transistor radio helps hurricane victims stay informed about weather news and storm developments.

AXE
The attic is the highest point in many homes. Many attics do not have windows. If floodwaters rise to the attic, people need an axe to break through the roof to survive.

SURVIVING THE STORM

IRON WILL STATS

Only three **Category 5** hurricanes have hit the US since 1900—the Labor Day Hurricane in 1935, Hurricane Camille in 1969, and Hurricane Andrew in 1992.

Tropical **Cyclone Olivia** struck Australia in 1996 with the fastest wind speeds ever measured on Earth's surface—**253 miles** (407 km) per hour.

The Great Hurricane of 1780 is believed to be the deadliest hurricane in recorded history. The 18th-century monster storm killed more than **20,000** when it struck the Caribbean.

About **20 percent** of the people living in Honduras were homeless after Hurricane Mitch hit in October 1998. Mitch killed between **11,000 and 18,000** people.

Six out of the **15** hurricanes of 2005 made landfall in the US, killing **1,518** people.

Hurricane season in the Atlantic Ocean usually runs from June 1 to November 30. An unnamed hurricane that formed on March 7, 1908, was the **only** hurricane every recorded in March.

The Atlantic Ocean hurricane to form the latest in the year was **Hurricane Alice**. Alice formed on December 31, 1954.

On average, **10 tropical storms** form each year. Of those 10 storms, only about 6 become hurricanes, and 5 of those make landfall somewhere in the US each year.

SURVIVING THE STORM 39

DEADLY STORMS

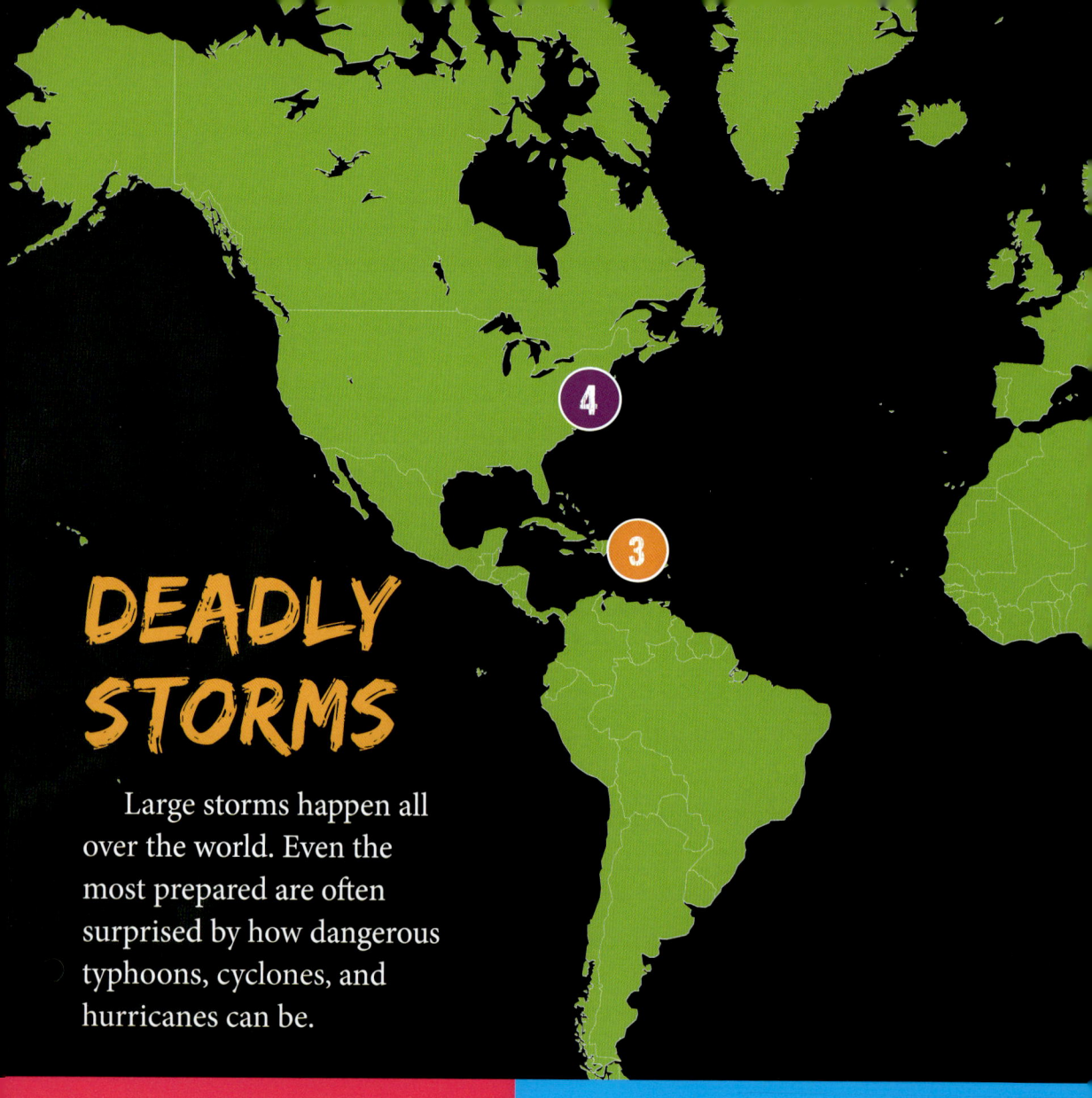

Large storms happen all over the world. Even the most prepared are often surprised by how dangerous typhoons, cyclones, and hurricanes can be.

1. HUGLI RIVER CYCLONE

Ganges River Delta

This huge storm made landfall on October 11, 1737. It is considered one of the deadliest natural disasters of all time. About 15 inches (38 cm) of rain fell in just a 6-hour period. Between 300,000 and 350,000 people died.

2. HAIPHONG TYPHOON

Gulf of Tonkin

In 1881, a large typhoon devastated the coastline of Vietnam. About 300,000 people died because of the storm and flooding. It is thought that thousands of people died after the storm due to disease and starvation because aid could not reach them fast enough.

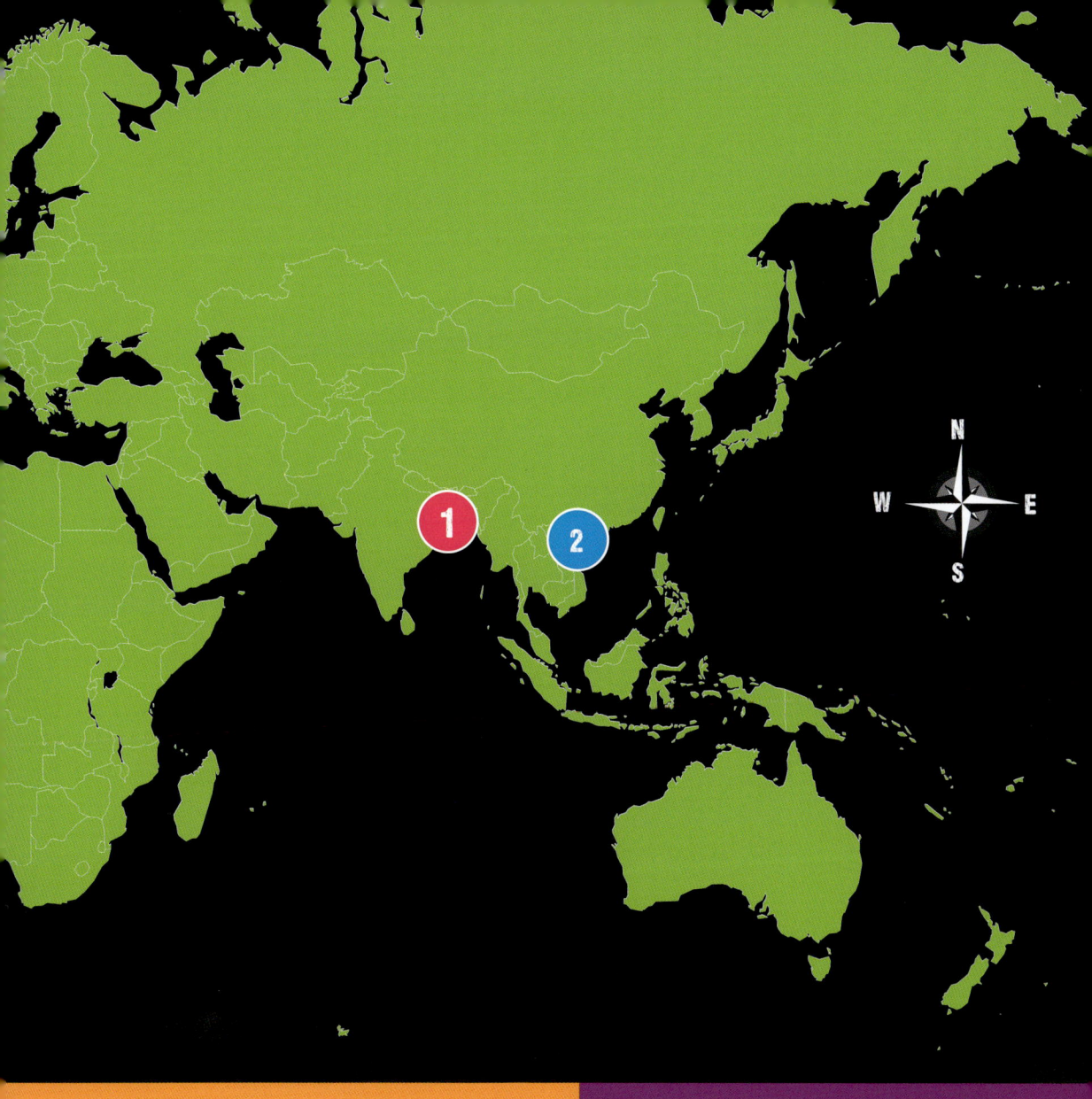

3. HURRICANE MARIA

Puerto Rico

By the time Hurricane Maria hit Peurto Rico in September 2017, it was a Category 4 storm. It was the strongest storm to hit the island in more than 80 years. Much of the island was without power for months after the storm. About 3,000 people died.

4. HURRICANE SANDY

Eastern Seaboard of the US

Hurricane Sandy is one of the most expensive hurricanes in history. The hurricane affected 24 states between October 22 to 29, 2012, with the most damage in New Jersey and New York. The cost totaled $68.7 billion.

SURVIVING THE STORM

IRON WILL

Hurricanes are dangerous and—in many cases—deadly. For many reasons, people might not be able to prepare for a hurricane before it arrives. The storm may move in so quickly that they don't have time to get ready. When this happens, people will need to follow a plan. They will need to gather supplies quickly. Or they will need to leave and go to a shelter. Family members, friends, and even strangers can come together to help each other survive a hurricane. Most importantly, people will need an iron will to survive a monster storm.

During Hurricane Katrina, many people were rescued from their roofs as flooding threatened their homes and lives.

SURVIVING THE STORM

QUIZ

1 How many people were ordered to evacuate before Hurricane Katrina?

2 How did Jaimie Cummings and her mother escape New Orleans?

3 How did Annie and Greg Smith make it to the hospital?

4 How did Lance Pasi contact his mother after Typhoon Yolanda?

5 Why didn't the people of Galveston, Texas, know that a hurricane was headed their way?

6 What is a hurricane warning?

7 What tool is needed to help people who are trapped in an attic without windows?

8 Which cyclone is considered the deadliest natural disaster of all time?

ANSWERS

1. About 1.2 million
2. On a police boat
3. On a dump truck
4. He texted her.
5. They didn't have the technology we have today to know when a strong storm is coming.
6. A hurricane warning means that hurricane conditions are expected in an area in 36 hours.
7. An axe
8. The Hugli River Cyclone of 1737

Imagine that you are under a hurricane warning. That means that weather forecasters believe you have only 36 hours before hurricane conditions reach where you live. Write a three-paragraph disaster plan. Answer these questions:

1. How will you prepare the inside of your home? What food supplies will you gather? What medical supplies will you need? What tools and items, such as flashlights and flares, will you need to stay safe inside your house?

2. How will you prepare the outside of your home? Items such as window shutters and patio furniture need to be secured or put away. Gas-powered generators and grills cannot be used inside or they will cause carbon monoxide poisoning. Where will you put these items so that they can be used safely in an emergency?

3. How will you evacuate with your family, if that becomes necessary? How can you check with local authorities to find out about official evacuation routes? Do you know the locations of emergency shelters in your community? What will you do with your pets?

Share your disaster plan with your friends and classmates. Did they write about something that you hadn't thought of? Did your ideas help them improve their disaster plans? Rewrite your disaster plan using the ideas that you and your friends shared with one another.

SURVIVING THE STORM

GLOSSARY

evacuate: to leave a dangerous place

flare: a fire or blaze of light used to send a signal or attract attention

impassable: not able to be passed, traveled, or crossed

iron will: having a strong feeling that you are going to do something and that you will not allow anything to stop you

meteorologist: a scientist who studies weather and weather patterns

refugee: a person who is a victim of a natural or human-made disaster and has no place to live

sterile: clean of bacteria

storm surge: a rising of the sea as a result of atmospheric pressure changes and wind associated with a storm

technology: tools and knowledge used to meet a need or solve a problem

torrent: a strong, fast-moving stream of water; a flood

transportation: a way to get from one place to another, usually in a vehicle of some sort

READ MORE

Challoner, Jack. *Eyewitness Hurricane & Tornado.* DK Publishing: New York, 2014.

Koontz, Robin Michal. *What Was Hurricane Katrina?* What Was? New York: Grosset & Dunlap, 2015.

Kostigen, Thomas. *Extreme Weather: Surviving Tornadoes, Sandstorms, Hailstorms, Blizzards, Hurricanes, and More!* Washington, DC: National Geographic, 2014.

Shotz, Jennifer Li. *Hero: Hurricane Rescue.* New York: Harper, 2017.

Tarshis, Lauren. *I Survived Hurricane Katrina, 2005.* I Survived. New York: Scholastic, 2011.

INTERNET SITES

http://www.weatherwizkids.com/?page_id=58
Learn more about hurricanes, including hurricane stages, safety, and evacuation tips.

https://www.weather.gov/safety/hurricane-ww
Find out the differences between official hurricane watches and hurricane warnings.

http://www.weatherquestions.com/What_causes_hurricanes.htm
Read about how storms are formed and the different categories of hurricanes.

https://eo.ucar.edu/kids/dangerwx/hurricane3.htm
Learn how hurricanes form and what causes storm surge.

INDEX

Atlantic Ocean 7, 13, 22, 39

evacuation 5, 8, 9, 19, 34

FEMA 9
flooding 5, 7, 8, 13, 14, 15, 16, 19, 20, 25, 26, 36, 37, 40, 43

Great Galveston Hurricane 24–29

Haiphong Typhoon 40
Houston, Texas 12, 13, 14, 16, 17, 28
Hugli River Cyclone 40
Hurricane Harvey 12–17
Hurricane Katrina 6–11, 30–35, 43
Hurricane Maria 41
Hurricane Sandy 41

meteorologists 5, 7, 25, 34

New Orleans, Louisiana 6, 7, 8, 10, 11

Ocean Springs, Mississippi 30, 31, 35

Pacific Ocean 22
Philippines 18, 19, 23

Red Cross 10

storm surge 7, 10, 20, 26, 31, 33, 35
Super Typhoon Yolanda 18–23
supplies 14, 28, 36, 42